FILTHY LITTLE THINGS

FILTHY LITTLE THINGS

JACK ZIEGLER

1981 DOLPHIN BOOKS
Doubleday & Company, Inc.
Garden City, New York

BOOK DESIGN BY SYLVIA DEMONTE-BAYARD

A DOLPHIN BOOK
Doubleday & Company, Inc.

ISBN: 0-385-17517-5
Library of Congress Catalog Card Number 80–2884

PRINTED IN THE UNITED STATES OF AMERICA
FIRST EDITION

For Jessica, Benjamin, and Max

INTRODUCTION

Some years ago, in San Francisco, my wife started hearing "rats" in the walls of our apartment. I insisted that they were not rats at all, but merely "something else," and that we therefore had nothing to fear. But women are funny, and she had me go upstairs to see our landlord, Marco, who dealt on the side in drugs, black market cigarettes, and babies. I asked him nicely to get an exterminator before the so-called rats came hopping out of the drainpipes to eat up our month-old baby, but he and his wife were in the middle of dinner (probably baby harp seal), and they didn't appreciate being disturbed. Marco adjusted his shoulder holster, spat some tiny bones from his mouth, and asked, "How would you like your nose exterminated?" He laughed mirthlessly, poking his wife in the ribs. Then he menaced me with his butter knife and told me to have it out with the little buggers myself, like a man. Realizing that Marco wasn't entirely sympathetic to our plight, I left him, the seal grease glistening brightly down his hairy Mafioso chest, before he could whip out any further snappy patter.

I was depressed. I had no money and felt trapped like a rat—or possibly "something else." Here we were, living in Hell's Kitchen West with Adolf Hitler, Jr., who, along with his black marketeering, moonlighted as a hit man for the Tong. And we couldn't even lie down on the floor to die without getting soaked, because there was no foundation in the house and much of the floor was simply bare ground with boards and carpet remnants strewn helter-skelter over it. The front yard was mud with a four-by-four blue concrete pond sunk into it, which Marco kept stocked with the few mutant catfish he managed to hook every weekend from a mile or so downstream from the Agent Orange Chemical Plant in San José. The fish never lasted more than a day or two: if the stagnant water in the pond didn't get them, the local cats did. Nearby lay a bleached cow skull, possibly the remnants of a former pet that the cats had also gotten to. The sound of gunfire and the ecstatic screams of the robust neighborhood floozies would echo through the streets at night as we huddled in our tiny bedroom hoping for a glimpse of America's sweetheart, Mary Tyler Moore, on our fuzzy little TV screen. No wonder my wife jumped at the opportunity of panicking over "rats" inside her purple-painted walls.

And so.

And so we decided to leave our little paradise at the south end of Baghdad-by-the-Bay. We moved to a slightly less tacky building, on Stanyan Street—I think it was called the Grateful Dead Arms—where the patchouli-scented landlord wore flowers, at times plastic flowers, in his hair and was willing to, like, give us our first month rent-free, man, if we would just, you know, kind of paint the apartment, oh wow, ceilings and all cabinets included of course, ourselves, you dig? This sounded fine to me, since my salary at the time was about eleven dollars a week.

Before we painted, though, we discovered that the apartment was also a rather good novel—the tale of a storm-tossed relationship, begun on a sea of joy and ended on the shoals of deceit and despair. Written on the living room wall, above where the sofa had once stood, was the concise first chapter. Written in the deft, bold strokes of the artist's initial inspiration (although in what I felt were ill-chosen two-foot-high red-crayoned block letters) were the words "Welcome to Your Humble Abode." On the door leading out to the hallway we found the impassioned, but well-edited, Chapters II through XXVI: "Babycakes, Don't Leave Me Now." Down the hall lay the bedroom, and therein the startling, though perhaps inevitable, denouement. Emblazoned the length of two entire walls, in lettering of a staggering size and yet with an alarming precision of thought, was this: "Fuck You and Your Ohio Bitch." In rapt exhaustion and with the ecstasy that sometimes comes with literacy, we donned our smocks. We knew our work was cut out for us. Two coats at least.

There are those who say we should have left the walls as they were, that we should have left the "art" and had an expert come in once a year to restore it. But no, we painted it over and didn't once look back. We stayed for our free month, at the end of which my wife heard something funny under the refrigerator.

And so.

And so we moved back East, where we had two more kids and got a dog and bought some filthy little things. I became a cartoonist and did this book, and we never had another moment's trouble for the rest of our lives.

Until yesterday, that is, when I thought I heard something funny in a murky, little-traveled corner of our attic.

J.Z.

PROLOGUE

ARRIVALS
PESTILENCE 4:02
FAMINE 4:15
MARTIAL LAW 4:21
TRIPLE LOCKS 5:00
UNEMPLOYMENT 5:20
INFLATION 5:32
SHORTER SUMMERS 5:43
LONGER ZIP CODES 5:46
PLASTIC SILVERWARE 6:01
DEPARTURES
GOOD TASTE 3:32
SLEIGH RIDES 3:49
ALL-BEEF BURGERS 4:25
HAPPINESS 5:11
SECURITY 5:15
FRIENDLY LOAN COMPANIES 5:58
WARM BLANKETS 6:10
HARDWOOD FLOORS 6:15
HOMEMADE ICE CREAM 6:31
ZIEGLER

1 TUESDAY

SAMMY DAVIS, JR., DIALS A WRONG NUMBER.

THE WAKER-UPPER
ZIEGLER
ZIEGLER

LOTS OF IMPORTANT INFORMATION THAT YOU HAVE TO KNOW
GOSSIP, RUMORS & WACKY STUNTS
ZIEGLER

Brand X
ZIEGLER

"Might I point out, Sergeant Drago, that we had a Hawaiian luau just last year, whereas it's been three years since we've had a Las Vegas Nite?"

REVOLUTION...
TIME TO GET UP, HONEY. THERE IS MUCH WORK TO BE DONE.
Che Lives
BOYCOTT LETTUCE
UP THE PEOPLE!
AGH. IS IT MONDAY AGAIN ALREADY?
...IT'S AN EIGHT-HOUR-A-DAY, FIVE-DAY-A-WEEK JOB.
ZIEGLER

“What’s good today, Eddie?”

EGGS OVER EASY,
A SIDE OF BACON,
TOAST WITH GRAPE JAM,
AND A REGULAR
COFFEE.
HERE COMES BREAKFAST!

THE
NOWHERE
HILTON
ZIEGLER

HURTLING TOWARD AN
APPOINTMENT WITH...
BUS
STOP
...DESTINY!!!
ZIEGLER

"No, I'm sorry, I don't have a dime to spare. I did, however, see one lying in the gutter not two blocks back."

LONG AFTER THE DEMISE OF MING THE MERCILESS...
...FLASH AND DALE CONTINUED TO VACATION ON THE PLANET MONGO.
ZIEGLER

"Liverwurst is down an eighth, egg–salad is up two and a half, and peanut–butter–and–jelly remains unchanged."

"Might I recommend the cud?"

HOW I MADE MY FIRST $8,000,000

ZIEGLER
ILLEGAL ALIENS
GAZETTE
ANOTHER REASON WHY
THEY'RE ILLEGAL.

ZIEGLER

INTERPRETER
1.

2.

5.

3.
4.
6.
7.
ZIEGLER

All my best, Lassie
Get well soon! -Lassie
warmest regards, Lassie
Have fun, Love, Lassie
DOGGIE TREETS
DOGGIE TREETS
LASSIE'S STUNTDOG
ZIEGLER

TROUBLE AHEAD

AN ACTOR PREPARES.

R-R-

R-R-R-R-R-

R-R-R-R-R-R-R-
R-R-R-R-R-R-R-
R-R-R-R-R-R-R-

R-RING!

H-H-H-H-H-H-H-H-

"I brought you up here today, son, because I wanted you to get a feel for the scope of this damned thing."

HILLDALE
Outlaw Commuters
ZIEGLER

THE HOLY MAN OF MALIBU BEACH

SENTIMENTS OF A LOST GENERATION

"All characters in this book are fictional, and any resemblance to persons, living or dead, is purely coincidental—with the exception of Mary Alice Keller, who never returned my phone call."

"Finally, Liebchen! Amerika!"

"Let's hope, Lucille, that our decision hasn't been too hasty."

"I'll bet he gets a great big kick out of making us look like assholes."

LOCAL MAIL
OUT-OF-TOWN MAIL
TOXIC CHEMICAL WASTE
ZIEGLER

"I can't alk-tay ow-nay."

JUST BEFORE THE PLAGUE OF THE FROGS AND LOCUSTS.

"Bob. Bob, Bob, Bob, Bob, Bob. Bob. Bob, Bob, Bob. Bob, Bob. Bob. Bob, you're fired."

2 NOON

3 LATER THAT SAME DAY

"It was the best of times, it was the worst of times– Hey! I'm talking to you! It was the best of times . . ."

"I coulda been a contender, Charlie. I coulda been somebody, instead of a snail, which is what I am . . ."

"Oil, oil, oil! Doesn't anyone ever talk about baseball anymore?"

Apr. 21 (UPI)—One of America's most beloved poets was struck down at his home today by deadly microwaves emanating from . . .

ZIEGLER
MERRILL LYNCH, PIERCE, FENNER & SMITH & MICK JAGGER
still only $1.99
ZIEGLER
Escape From 199

“. . . Meanwhile, back at Cindy’s apartment . . .”

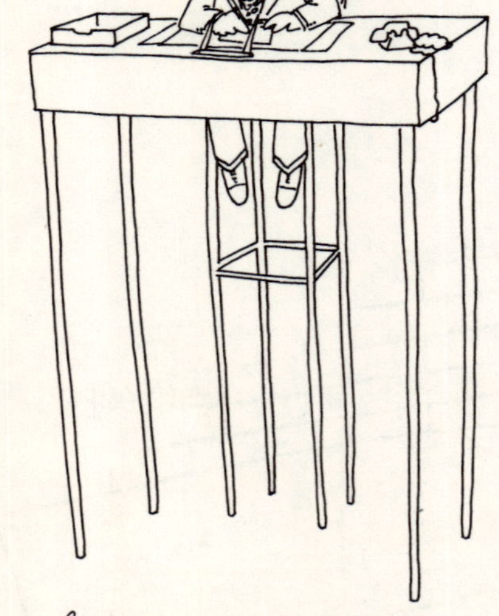

“If it isn’t one thing, it’s another–huh, Tom?”

THE COUNT OF MONTE CRISTO
THE LAST OF THE MOHICANS
THE MAN IN THE IRON MASK
THE COUNT OF MONTE CRISTO
THE LAST OF THE MOHICANS
THE MAN IN THE IRON MASK
THE COUNT OF MONTE CRISTO
THE LAST OF THE MOHICANS
THE MAN IN THE IRON MASK
ZIEGLER

THE FURTHER ADVENTURES OF
FLASH GORDON
BY 1997, MING THE MERCILESS WAS FORCED TO SEEK A COURT ORDER FROM THE SUPREME COURT TO HAVE FLASH AND HIS BY-THEN CONSIDERABLE ENTOURAGE THROWN OFF THE PLANET MONGO.
ZIEGLER

1
2
3
WHY DOES THE CHICKEN TO BE CROSSING THE STREET?
NO SPATZKI CHOKI.
BECAUSE HE HAS TO BE GETTING ACROSS THE ROAD!
KEH KEH KEH.
HOW IS IT THAT THE FIREMAN IS WEARING ALSO THE RED BREECH HALTERS?
NO SPATZKI CHOKI.
FOR THE TROUSERS!
KEH KEH KEH!
WHAT IS BLACK, WHITE, RED, AND ALL OVER?
NO SPATZKI CHOKI.
WALL STREET JOURNAL!
KEH KEH KEH.
THE BERLITZ SCHOOL OF PARTY JOKES

NEW YORK STREET GANGS
A RANDOM SAMPLING
THE ACCORDICREEPS
NEW YORK CITY
HELL'S PASTRIES
VICIOUS TOASTERS
The Savage Towels
SATAN'S GALOSHES
THE BROADWAY MELODIES OF 1938
ZIEGLER

Battlestar Galápagos

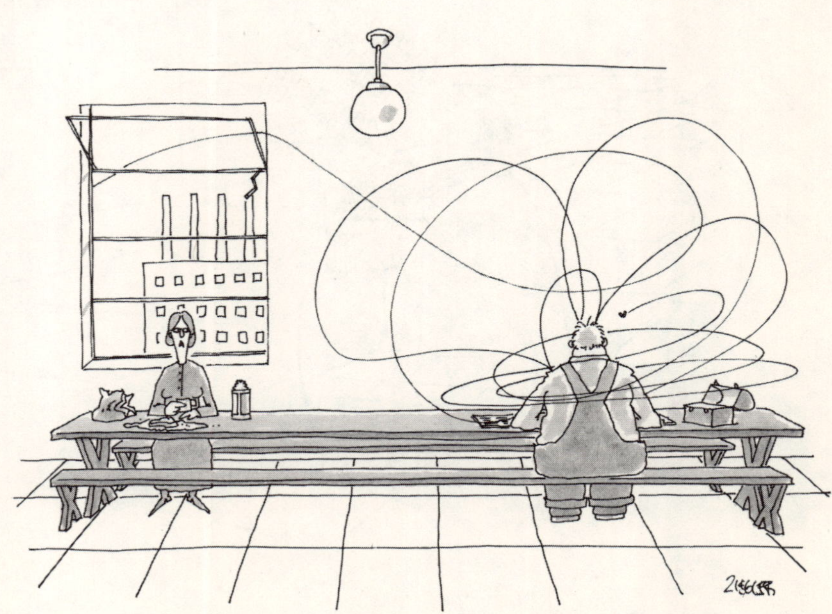

"This may be none of my business, Mr. Sutter, but that fly is deliberately trying to humiliate you."

MUNCH
MUNCH
MUNCH
POPCORN
ZIEGLER

"Hey, you guys, Heil Hitler, huh?"

"Victory. Peace. Two. All I know is it drives them bananas."

"Hello, Mom? It's me. Punk rock just died, so I'll be home in about fifteen minutes, O.K.?"

"They've always been such nice neighbors—friendly, quiet. Up until today, of course."

AN UNFORTUNATE DIRECTION
FOR MECCA
ZIEGLER

eggs
bread
liverwurst
coffee
cigarettes
2 milk
sound effect.
I JUST CAN'T WAIT FOR MY DATE TONIGHT WITH MELISSA.
ZIEGLER

"More crowd noise, O.K., Phil?"

"Hey, look who's here! Come on out here, you nut, you crazy guy!"

"You had to be there."

"It's Swedish, but it's very, very, very funny."

NO HARMFUL SIDE EFFECTS
WELL, HARDLY ANY.
TRUTH IN ADVERTISING
ZIEGLER

IN THE LAND OF THE KISSING FOOLS
ZIEGLER

"Hey! Just because I'm an illegal alien doesn't mean that my beads are no good!"

THRUST...

... A TIME EXPOSURE

TOURIST
CLASS
ZIEGLER

ZIEGLER

A NEARSIGHTED STUDENT FROM PEKING,
CONFUSED WHEN HIS FEET BEGAN SQUEAKING,
CLIMBED UP ON A BOX
TO GET CLOSE TO HIS SOX,
BUT NEVER FOUND WHAT HE WAS SEEKING.
A MIDNIGHT READING FROM CHAIRMAN MAO'S LONG-SUPPRESSED, BUT OFT-QUOTED, "LITTLE GREEN BOOK"
ZIEGLER

THE DARK SIDE OF
THE LONE RANGER
WHAT AM I TALKING, TONTO? CHOPPED LIVER? NO! I'M TALKING SILVER BULLETS!
I DON'T CARE HOW YOU GET THEM, DAMMIT — JUST GET THEM!

OFFICIAL OK

OFFICIAL OK

NEMESIS OF THE SUPERHEROES

35¢

ZIEGLER

IN THIS ISSUE:
CALVES' LIVER,
LIMA BEANS,
AND SQUASH!

"I said, 'Heil Hitler,' mein Liebchen. Sometimes it means hello . . . and sometimes it means goodbye."

CATSUP

Oooo
Four score
and seven years
ago BASKETBALL
our fathers brought
forth on BASKETBALL
this continent a new
nation BASKETBALL con-
ceived BASKETBALL in
liberty BASKETBALL and
ded— BASKETBALL BASKETBALL
BASKETBALL BASKETBALL!

Last row: Scott, Jennifer, Jennifer, Scott, Jennifer, Jennifer, Scott, Scott *Middle row:* Jennifer, Jennifer, Scott, Scott, Jennifer, Jennifer, Scott, Jennifer, Scott *Front row:* Jennifer, Scott, Scott, Jennifer, Mrs. Wanda Projhieki, Scott, Scott, Scott, Scott

"I hadn't read in the columns, Larry, that you had turned mean."

SEMI-LUXURY LINER

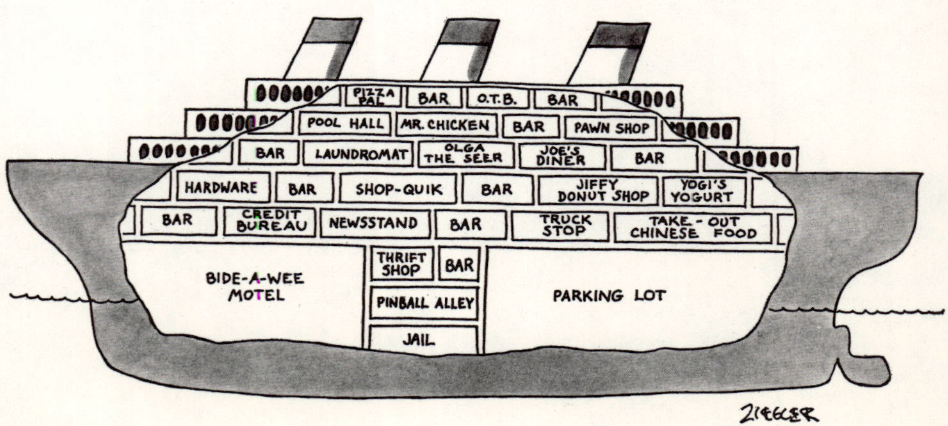

INDENTURED ANGELS
ZIEGLER

"...SUDDENLY IT HIT ME – I
WAS THEIR PRISONER!"
ZIEGLER

SHORE
NUFF!
MR. ABNER YOKUM
ZIEGLER
FREE AT LAST TO PURSUE HIS
TRUE CALLING — INSURANCE.

"But the *people*, Your Majesty! The *people* are not happy."

CORPORATE WARFARE
ZIEGLER

"South Moluccan extremists!"

BONK
YIPES!
BONK
*YIPES!
ZIEGLER

I settled into the plush violet seat, ~~by~~ my back to the great window overlooking Cold Spring Harbor. The famous man offered me a cup of tea, which I gratefully accepted. His vast mustaches drooped nearly to his ~~breast~~ ~~chest~~ ~~stomach~~ lapels, his unruly white hair ~~dancing~~ ~~prancing~~ shimmering in the noonday sun. (?) His noble presence seemed to fill the room ~~like a~~ ~~much as a~~ ~~not unlike a~~. My soul ~~wafted aloft~~ soared as he spoke. "So you want to be a writer," he said. "Yes," I stammered, "I ~~believe~~ fancy I do."

ZIEGLER

The New Iconography

THE OMEN

PLUMBING TROUBLE OF THE GODS
ZIEGLER

"Stop looking at me! How do you expect me to sentence you when you keep looking at me?"

Nov. 28 (UPI)—At his office in the capital city, the world's most powerful dictator greets the world's funniest stand-up comic. (Official Government Photo)

THE
AMAZINGLY INEXPENSIVE
MOVING CO.
ZIEGLER

"Those? Oh, things to do, random thoughts, and some ideas for my novel."

"This one might be a bit out of your price range, sir. It costs eighteen zillion dollars."

4 4:36 P.M., E.S.T.

"Wake up, Captain. Time to go down with the ship."

"And, finally, tonight's rerun of 'Kojak' has been canceled so that we can bring you an expanded, ninety-minute version of 'Soap.' "

NEW L.A. SUBDIVISION

Our Song

"Anyone want my olive?"

PANDERING TO INTELLECTUALS

DIRTY WORDS FROM AROUND THE WORLD

"I don't know about you, but I'm getting soaked."

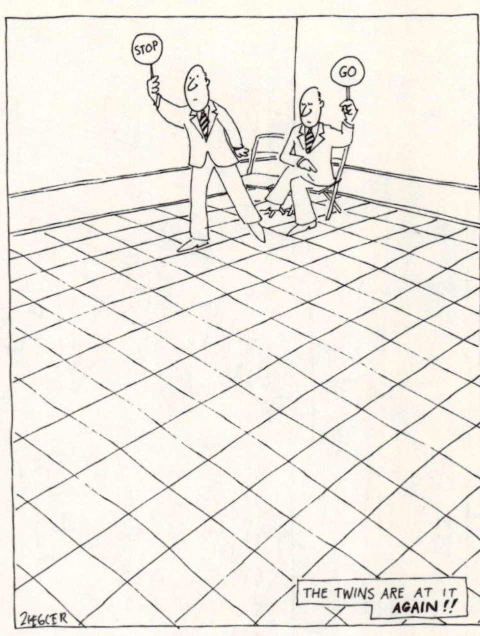

SAMMY'S VALE O'TEARS SHOPPE
WOW! GIANT 16-OZ. BOTTLE OF AGONY only 99¢!
GRIEF $1.69 per LB.
BIG BAG OF ASSORTED WOES! only $3.98!
LOOK! TORMENT Now only 79¢
DISTRESS! PRICED TO SELL @ 3 for $1.00
NOW IN BLOOM! MELANCHOLIA $2.49
6-PACK OF DREAD! only $1.79!
A VERY GOOD DEAL ON THE BLUES! JUST ASK SAMMY!
ZIEGLER

3 SCENES FROM ARMAND'S DAY

"That's *Ms.* Blessed Virgin Mary to you, fella!"

Ming the Merciless and his twin brother, Ming the Merciful, at Bridalveil Fall, Yosemite Nat'l Park, 1939. (Photo courtesy of F. Gordon)

"Come on, pal, give me a break."

In the Caviar Fields

"Say hi to the famous Mona Lisa."

"No problem. I merely fell harmlessly into the ocean."

"You kall this klean?"

ZIEGLER
WALTER B. MONTAGUE III (CHAIRMAN OF THE BOARD OF AMALGAMATED OIL, PRESIDENT OF THE AMERICAN COUNCIL ON ECONOMIC PRIORITIES, PRESIDENT OF THE SOCIETY FOR A BETTER WORLD, BOARD MEMBER OF SAVE-THE-TREES, FORMER AMBASSADOR TO FRANCE, FORMER MAYOR OF HACKENSACK, NEW JERSEY, ADVISOR TO KINGS AND PRESIDENTS, PHI BETA KAPPA-HARVARD UNIV., FATHER OF THREE) ATTEMPTS TO ESCAPE FROM HIS SHADOW.

PATRONS OF THE ARTS
ZIEGLER

"This is a lot harder on me. I'm a corporate person."

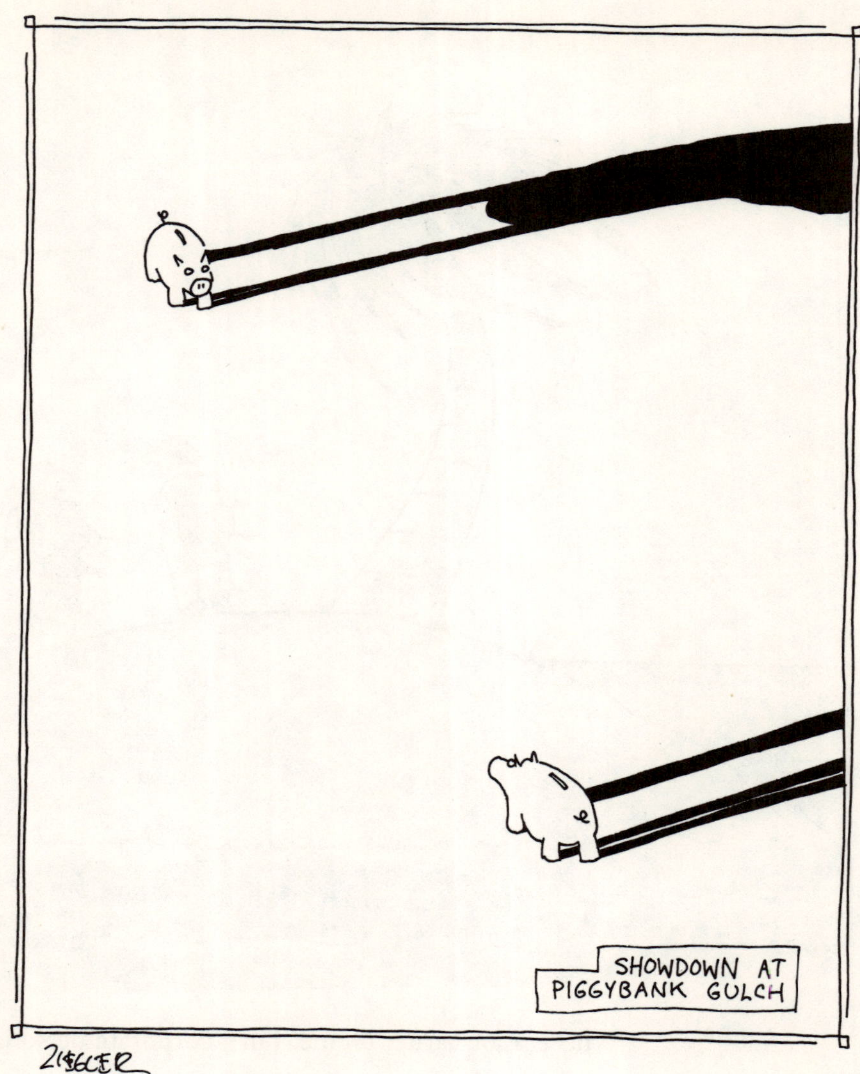
SHOWDOWN AT
PIGGYBANK GULCH

THE PACKAGING OF A. HITLER

(THE REJECTS)

ZIEGLER

ZIEGLER

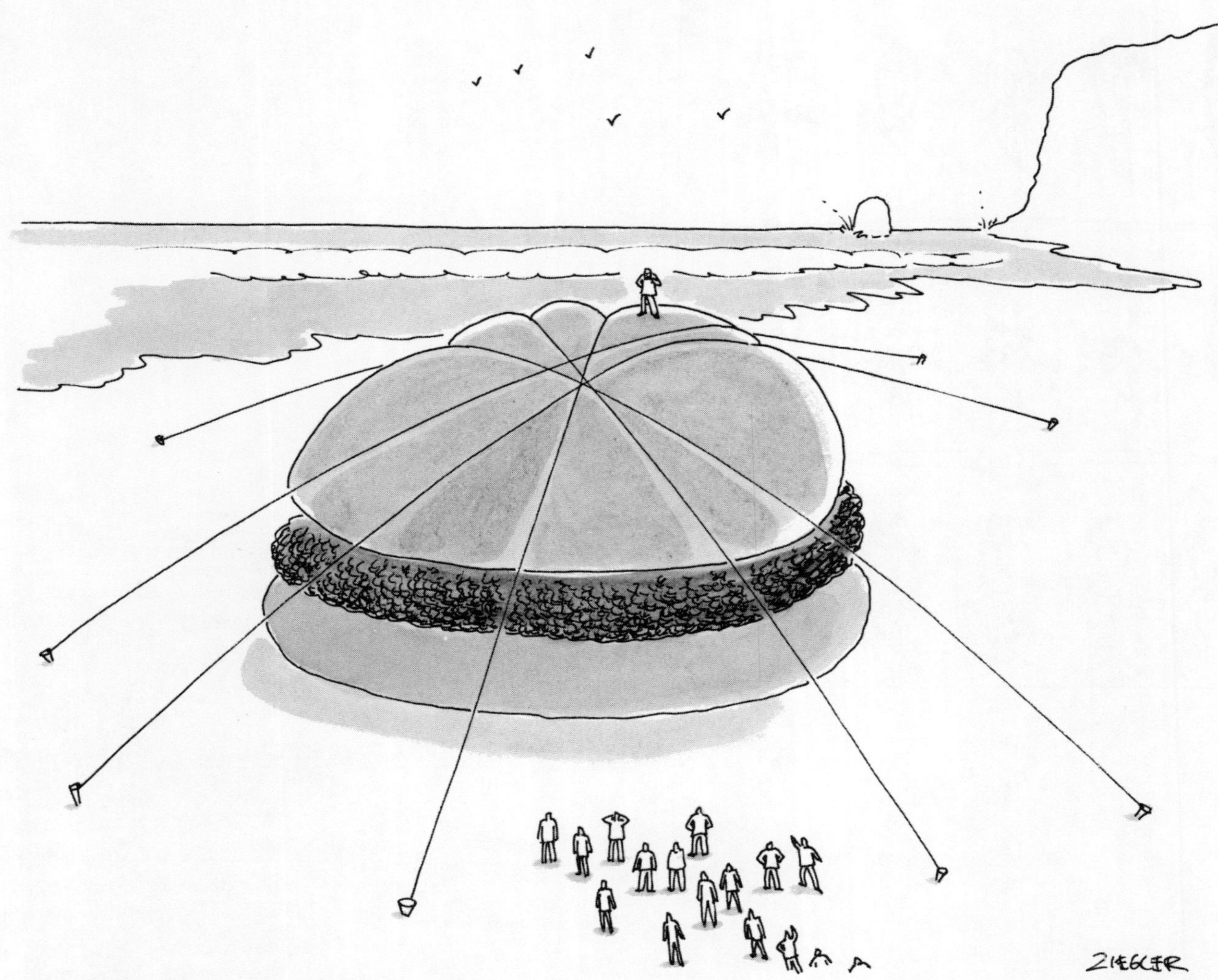
ZIEGLER

I HAVEN'T THE SLIGHTEST IDEA OF WHAT I'M TALKING ABOUT.
VOTE
MAN OF COURAGE

FLASH, DARLING, WONDERFUL TO HEAR FROM YOU.
UPDATE ON MING THE MERCILESS.

"Good Lord! Is summer over already?"

"The blues have been good to us, Binky."

Budget Munchies

ZIEGLER

Peanut Butter and Jelly Sandwich Quiche

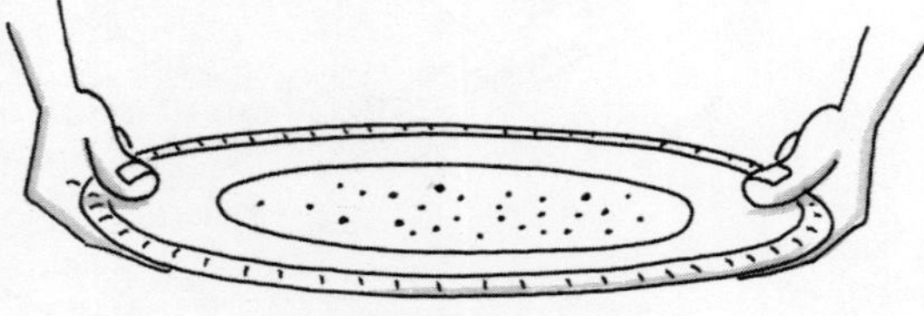

Diet Nibbles

Devilled Ice-Cream Cones

Carved Logs of Jerky de Boeuf

Ravioli Puff Fondue

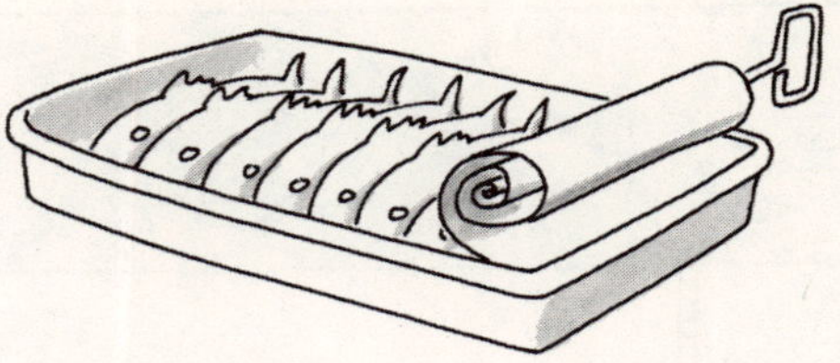

Fish Quickies

Assorted Snacks

Swedish Furballs

MAYBE.
PERHAPS.
JARGON
ZIEGLER

LONG, LONG AGO IN A GALAXY FAR, FAR AWAY...
HEY NONNY NONNY NONNY?
HEY NONNY NONNY NO!
ZIEGLER
HEREDITY
ZIEGLER

YOU CALL THAT A SANDWICH?
YIPES!
WHOOPS!
$34 ??
HEY, THAT'S MINE!
UH-OH!
$35 ???
OHHHHHH NOOOOOO!
THE DOG ATE MY WHAT-T-T?
The Sitcom Family
ZIEGLER

TAX TIME FOR THE MONGOL HORDE

At the Coney Island Hotel

HONK

BEEP
THE MAN WHO COULD COMMUNICATE WITH GEESE

NEW MIRACLE PRODUCT
MOSES

"Fleetwood Mac, they say that you possess greatness. But I do not understand you."

5 IS THIS THE END OF RICO?

WOWIE ZOWIE.
SCOOBY DOOBY DOO.
HEY NONNY NONNY NO.
OOPS-A-DAISY.
HUBBA HUBBA.
OO BOP SHA-BAM!
SCUDDA HO!
SCUDDA HEY!
HUNKY DORY.
OKEY DOKE.
HOTSY TOTSY.
THE JUNGLE NEVER SLEEPS.
ZIEGLER

THANK YOU FOR WATCHING AND GOOD NIGHT.
HEY! WHAT MAKES HIM THINK WE WERE WATCHING?
WE WEREN'T WATCHING!
SOMEBODY CALL HIM UP QUICK AND TELL HIM WE WEREN'T WATCHING!
ZIEGLER

VONNEGUT FUNNIES
ZIEGLER
SO IT GOES.

"Could one of you guys pass the ketchup?"

The New York Times – Carnegie Hall Poll

"If there are no further questions, I shall proceed."

ZIEGLER

handsome moustache
luxuriant beard
unsightly facial hair
ZIEGLER

"We'll be back in a minute with Harlan Harris's Sports Extra, Jules Bernmeier and the weather, Jimmy Cunningham's Entertainment Plus, Judith Enright's Fashion Notes, Grady O'Toole's Celebrity Interview, Maria Dellago's Budget Center, Murray Vaughan's Mister Fix-It Shop, and me, Biff Brogan, with a note on the news."

SUBURBIA
No. 1
funnies
10¢
featuring:
TASTELESS TONY TERWILLIGER
THE BOOR OF LARCHMONT
SAY, FELLA, WHERE WERE YOU WHEN THEY HANDED OUT THE GUCCIS?
ISN'T HE AWFUL?!
ZIEGLER

HIYA,
SAILOR.
ZIEGLER
THE TRUTH ABOUT TINKER BELL

MEN

During the day he was a butcher of meats; but at night he became a man.

At the office he made important decisions and chased after leggy blonde secretaries; but at night he became a man.

ZOW
PINBALL

When they needed someone to lift large crates filled with nuts and bolts and big nameless metal objects, they called him; but at night he became a man.

PLEASE
STAY
TUNED

They had hired him to do a job and he carried it off without a hitch, emotionless, swift, silent, and... deadly; but at night he became a man.

ZIEGLER

"You scumbag."

I HAVE NOTHING TO SAY!
IT BEGAN WHEN I WAS A CHILD IN PARIS...
THE WINTERS WERE COLD BUT WE HAD EACH OTHER...
MAX THOUGHT WE WERE CRAZY...
I REMEMBER A LARGE PORTRAIT OF GRANDMOTHER ABOVE THE FIREPLACE...
LEMONADE UNDER THE SYCAMORES OUT BACK...
THAT WAS THE FIRST TIME I EVER SAW PAMELA...
WHEN I TURNED AROUND, THE OTHERS HAD ALREADY LEFT...
THOSE NIGHTS AT THE VILLA WERE, HOW CAN I EXPRESS IT?, IDYLLIC...
HE WAS MY FRIEND, OR SO I THOUGHT...
YOU'LL NEVER BREAK ME, COPPER!
ZIEGLER

". . . Carry the 4, carry the 4, carry the 4—4 and 7 is, is, is—4 and 7 is 8, 9, 10, 11—4 and 7 is 11. O.K. Now, 11 and 6 is . . ."

Origins of Tonto

HISTORY OF ROCK
1956
1961
1964
1968
1974
1979
ZIEGLER

"Norman Mailer, meet Gore Vidal. Ha-ha, just kidding."

"I LOVE LUCY —
THE MOTION PICTURE"

"Hey, hey, O.K.! How many of you have done *this?* You go to wash your hands and there's this piece of *spinach* stuck in the soap. Right? Right? And how about *this?* You fall out of bed in the middle of the night and when you wake up you can't figure out why the ceiling is so far away and the only logical explanation is that you've suddenly become the incredible shrinking man. Right? Recognize *that* one? Huh? Am I hitting home? Huh? Huh?"

Sitting In

KNOCK KNOCK.
WHO'S THERE?
ZIEGLER

"Stop complaining! You knew I was a nun when you married me!"

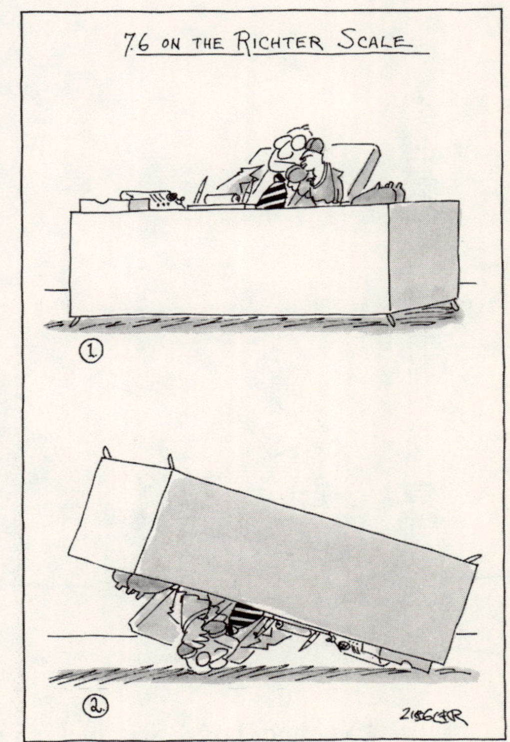

"Yoohoo, boys! Seig heil, or whatever!"

SUDDENLY I AWOKE AND SAID:
YAAAH!
...AFTER WHICH I WENT RIGHT BACK TO SLEEP.
ZIEGLER

BREAD AND WATER AND T.V. AND STEREO

No! **NO!**
NOT THE
NATIONAL ANTHEM!
NOT SO SOON!!
Villa
Maria
PIZZA
BURGER
KING
ZIEGLER

COMMIE

HEY! I KNOW THIS GUY!
SMALL WORLD
ZIEGLER

!!
I KNOW! I KNOW!
ZIEGLER

OLD SUPERHEROES' HOME
ZIEGLER

SUBTLE
Nuances
nasty
QUIRKS
ZIEGLER

"Thank God you're here. Walter has been Barry Manilowing us to death."

"Why, thank you. It becomes you, too."

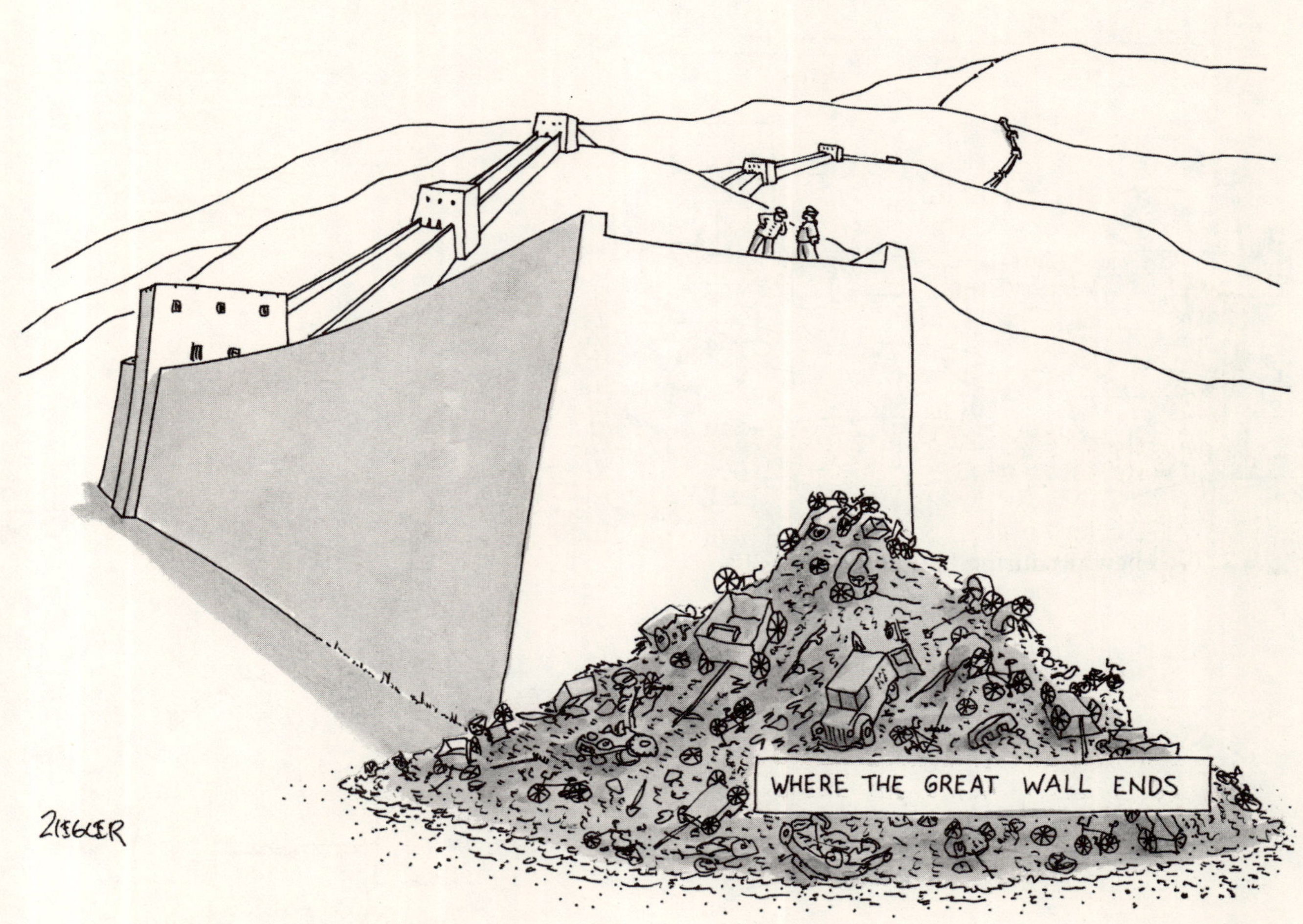
WHERE THE GREAT WALL ENDS
ZIEGLER

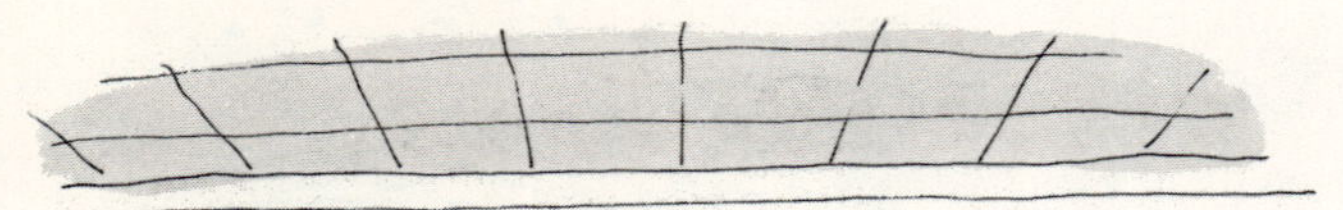

"No chewing during 'Autumn Leaves'!"

"Hiya, Johnny! Who are your guests tonight? Don Rickles? A funny man. A funny, funny, funny man. Charo? Hi, Charo! Love your hair. Gonna dance for us tonight, Charo? That's good! Glen Campbell? I love this guy. I'm a rhinestone cowboy—right, Glen? Ha-ha-ha. Ha-ha-ha-ha. Carl Sagan? Whoops! You'll be on way past *my* bedtime, Carl. Say hi to Carl for me, though, will you, Johnny?"

EPILOGUE

"Thanks, baby. Ciao."